CULTURE DRIVEN RECRUITING

CULTURE DRIVEN RECRUITING

THERE IS NO "TALENT WAR" IF YOU ELIMINATE THE COMPETITION

Lee-Anne Edwards

Palmetto Publishing Group
Charleston, SC

Culture Driven Recruiting

First Edition

Printed in the United States

ISBN-13: 978-1-64111-163-8
ISBN-10: 1-64111-163-1

CONTENTS

FOREWORD

WE ARE GOING TO BECOME FAST FRIENDS.

Let's talk about you. You may be a salty, seasoned recruiter and an HR whisperer, or you may be new to the game - just dipping a toe into the choppy waters of recruiting. Regardless of where you are on your recruiting journey, this book can be for you. If you are looking for a better way to recruit you will find that here. If you are looking to find a way to automate your recruiting organically you have come to the right place. If you are an agency recruiter, I hope you can share this knowledge with your current and future clients much like we do at OneinaMil.

This won't be a fast process so get your head right. It won't be anything that you are expecting. I don't believe in fluff. Nor should you. I believe in efficiency and facts. You will not find any fluff in this book as nobody has time for that. Let's keep it simple friends.

Before we start, I only ask three things of you: that you absolutely love what you do; you are shamelessly seeking to break the chains of traditional recruiting; and you desperately want to recreate your recruiting process in the most innovative way.

Sound like you? Read on.

A little about me. I have been in recruiting for more than 15 years. During this stint, I have run the gamut. I have been an internal recruiter several times and currently I would categorize myself as an agency recruiter/Culture Development Strategist. I have been a part of the big corporate life and the five-person start-up's. I have seen some things and have some war stories to share, my friends. While, I still have a ton to learn on this journey we call life, I am excited to share what I have learned over the last decade and a half.

Recently, over the last few years I have even had a small soiree on screen as a part of several docufilms featuring recruiters from all over the world. A couple of years ago, I was asked to be a subject matter expert for the "Art of Recruiting" to discuss ever evolving ideas and trends in the industry. It was brilliant. People flew in from all over the world to be surrounded by recruiting guru's. Real talk, that was a top ten life experience for me.

Two Summers ago, I was able to be a contestant on the "Top Recruiter Four," a reality series filmed out of Miami. Highlight of that week? I slept in Jackie Chan's bed (no he was not in it) and we had professional chefs on-site, make-up artists, hair stylists and endless champagne. All joking aside you will have to feed me wine to get me to tell those stories, but what an epic ride. The friendships, colleagues and clients I came out of that show with you couldn't put a price tag on. A life experience it was. Unfortunately, the show ended up being full scripted by the time the full cast had arrived but have no fear, we made the best of

Jackie Chan's waterfront mansion. If you get crazy and want to catch a glimpse of these glory days you can catch them here: https://vimeo.com/137262085.

Bringing us full circle, I have had the pleasure of meeting and learning from a plethora of phenomenal recruiters over the years. My intention, however ambitious, is to pack all of this knowledge into one spot for all of you. I am hoping this book may be your quick go-to with answers to some hard questions, a little guidance for next steps, and possibly a pep talk in a pinch.

Here's the deal, I had a lot of help along the way - peppered with ideas and inspiration from the best in the business. I also had a killer mentor for the last decade who taught me every last thing he knew from real life experience in the realm of culture and recruiting. Today, my team and I work with organizations across the country on a simple mission: to build epic recruiting teams and amazing culture driven organizations. We are in the weeds, working day in and day out with HR Managers and recruiting experts to find those "one in a million" hires, learn how to keep them and here's the clincher, to have them help you recruit their "A player" friends.

All that to say, culture driven recruiting and more importantly culture driven organizational development is my passion and I'm excited to share it with you. I hope this book brings you some new perspective, starts a conversation or three, helps you usher in a shred of efficiency, exposes you to a new idea or two, makes you giggle, and, possibly, serves as a breath of fresh air in a space I find is all too often ridden with "we've always done it this way." Keep saying this out loud to yourself, "There is no talent war if you eliminate the competition."

So, dive on in. Open your mind and get ready. Toss this baby in your purse, have it in the front seat or keep it at your desk.

Special thanks to my astounding editors for pulling out or dubbing over all of my curse words and keeping this classy. If anyone wants the unedited version, hit me up at la.edwards@oneinamil.com.

In Shared Success,
LA

CHAPTER ONE

THE BACKGROUND STORY: HOW THE FLIT DID WE GET HERE?

"And then there is the most dangerous risk of all... the risk of spending your life not doing what you want on the bet you can buy yourself the freedom to do it later." - Randy Komisar

I have spent years facing the same problem throughout every industry. Finding good talent is hard. Finding ways to keep good talent remains even harder. I started OneinaMil almost five years ago for this very reason. There is a solid need out there to fix this broken work world we live in.

For too many decades work has flat out sucked. Work environments have sucked. The game has changed and the best part of my job is being able to be on the ground working with organizations all over the nation to help them recruit faster, better, cheaper, all by building a foundation to support it. If you build it, they will come. Trust me.

It's a wild world. We are in a tumultuous phase of redefining the American dream. So let's take eight steps back to understand the players in the current job market and how their life experience is influencing where we are today.

I'm looking at you, Baby Boomers (born between 1940s and mid-60s), who are currently having night sweats over will-we-won't-we social security and maybe pensions under threat of being eliminated or reduced. Many of you are still recovering from the crash in 2008 and retirement may seem like a pipe dream. Here's to you for getting up, clocking in, and going to the same job everyday to give your children a better life.

You were likely taught that a life-long career was the only way. You were told to stick to the grind day in and day out whether you liked it or not. They promised you, if you worked hard your whole life, secured that white-picket fence and paid for your kids' college then you had a sweet playdate waiting for you on your 70th birthday.

Here's what you probably did not do. You did not demand a healthier work environment because you might be fired. You did not stand up to your boss because you might be fired. You got pay raises annually on a predetermined percentage scale and did not dare ask for what you were worth because you might be fired. You were part of a protective machine that would love you back if you stayed the straight and narrow and did not rock the boat. Nobody is blaming you, you did what you thought was the right thing to do.

Success was owning a home, paying your bills and putting food on the table for your family. You had a road map and it all started with a 4-year college degree. All this to say, finding meaning and passion in your job wasn't the priority - it was all about staying the course because the course paid off. Right?

For us Gen Xer's (born between 60s and early 80s), we tried to take that roadmap from our Baby Boomer parents, but found that road to glory riddled with potholes. Many of us are juggling crippling debt from trying to buy our own white picket fence and are wondering how the ho-hos we will put our kids through college when we will be paying off our own student loans until the day we die.

We were told by our parents "get that 4-year degree, ANY degree, and you will get a stable job," only to find that a Bachelor's in the Mating Habits of Butterflies was not quite the launch pad for a career in Human Resources or entrepreneurship. No, Mating Habits of Butterflies was not my major. From 2000-2010, the market was inundated with graduates with degrees in sociology and liberal arts who just floundered. They realized this sacred roadmap might just lead to nowhere - staring down the harsh reality of an employer's market and uncertain financial future.

Most of our generation ended up going back to school for a trade or specialty to try and thin the competitive herd. However, this generation, we got a bit smarter when it came to our personal lives and started bucking the notion that we had to stay in a marriage that no longer added value to our life. For the first time, you started to see that frustration pivot into focus on the harsh reality that life is short and none of us make it out alive, so it's okay to be selfish about some things.

Now our biggest worries center around how we are going to support our parents financially when they can no longer work and shenanigans have hit the fan with their well-intentioned plans screwed six ways to

Sunday by the 2008 crash. We are a generation that started to question self-care, self-awareness and finding time to relax and enjoy existence. Many of us still stick with the 9 to 5 gig, but we haven't hitched our star to the traditional trajectory. Many of us are finding better ways to make a living so that we can spend more time with our children and (likely) second-round spouses.

Then we had the Millennials (born between 1980ish and 1995) who just set fire to the road map because none of it even started to work for them. Although I'm technically a Gen Xer, I identify more with the Millennial camp because I attribute them with being the disrupters. To know me is to love me, and I am disruptive. Being disruptive and sometimes taking that lonely, undefined path is what really gets me out of bed in the morning.

Millennials are disrupting everything we thought we knew about work/life balance. They took stock of marriage, children,and the white picket fence and said...why? They saw that it wasn't working for the last couple generations and decided to draw a new road map - for better or for worse.

This generation started to wait. Wait on marriage. Wait on kids. Wait on buying a home. Partially because many of these financial milestones became significantly harder to achieve in comparison to their parents path, but also because, well, they tend to want less strings. This gang shifted the priority from grinding to "living the best life" and started spending more on experiences over building wealth through possessions. They are also bringing a slow death to things like the Big Mac and paper napkins. They are teaching their children that experiences and memories win everyday all day against another new bike or doll that they so desperately don't need.

For better or worse, Millennials reevaluated and decided that if they were going to work for their entire lives then they were going to love it and feel some semblance of significance about it. Regrettably, retirement started to fall off the radar; possibly, because it seems so far out of reach for most or because YOLO. Why would we work ourselves to death so that when we are old, overweight, tired, and sore can only then enjoy the fruits of our labor. Um… no.

This generation started to ask for (expect?) fantastical notions like sabbaticals and working remotely and they do NOT feel bad about it. Down with the cube! These crazy kids want to work from boats, cars, hammocks, rooftops, airplanes, co-working spaces, or wherever there is wi-fi. They tend to value personal significance over salary - make no mistake, they still want that paper, but they also want to feel important and valued as an individual contributor.
The challenge with Millennials is that they don't often subscribe to company loyalty - mainly as a result of seeing their parents crash and burn trying to ride that wagon through to a so-called retirement. They tend to look at jobs like projects - committing to a year or two before moving on to the next shiny thing if they are unfulfilled or do not feel appreciated. They are hustlers who often rely on multiple revenue streams to make ends meet and battle back boredom. They know that if they can figure out a way for one of those revenue streams to make them money while they sleep, than they are optimizing at full capacity.

This squad gets a bad wrap for lack of work ethic and acting as if they are owed something; although I personally find this to be an exception and suspect it's more often a consequence of shallow cultures… more on that in a minute. Millennials are a lonelier group who crave flexibility and freedom - bringing them into the fold as a true team member is tough. Love them or hate them, Millenials want to be happy, engaged, adored and a contributor to something great - they are hungry to earn it, but will be just as quick to jump ship if you don't give it.

Looking forward, we have Gen Z (born after 1995) being groomed to take the workforce by storm making up a quarter of the U.S. population and projected to account for 40% of all consumers by 2020. While we may want to label them "zombies" and "screen addicts," we need to spend time understanding what they think, believe and desire since, they are in fact, our future.

This group is already asking - How can I work hard, but work less hours and make the most money doing something I love? They are second guessing a formal education. Why would I take classes and sink into student loan debt unless it's guaranteed to get me ahead? This generation is opting out of the non-guaranteed and wanting an alternative yesterday. Can you blame them? The reality is that they were raised with mini-computers in hand and are light-years faster than all of us on the tech front. Hell, the Snapchat user interface was not created for anyone but the Gen Z's. These kids know what they want, and they know how to get it. They have no fear. Kids, marriage, all of that is a strong maybe for this generation.

All this to say, if you are in human resources, starting up your own organization, recruiting for companies nationally, working as an internal recruiter, or anything in between, you need to know how these people tick and understand their why. You need to know what you do not know.

Everyday, OIAM is out in the field. We work hand in hand with organizations from coast to coast. Some are large. Some are small. But they all need the same thing - a talented team to hitch their star to. Although their structures and visions may be different, our clients call us for one of three reasons: either their culture is broken or they are just getting started and want to do it right, or their current recruiting team needs a serious makeover and they need top talent desperately.

So here it is. Now that you've sat through the how-we-got-here history lesson, let's talk about what to do about it...or with it. This is my why. Why do I hire on culture and how do I hire on culture fit? Some arguably say it's some subjective bullshit, but I say this is what gets me out of bed in the morning. The psychology behind the work we do is utterly fascinating.

Let's revisit our buddies, the Millennials. This generation understands self-awareness and how important finding yourself is to finding your optimal career. They will not settle for the best paying job - for many, money is fourth in line. They want more because they believe they deserve more. They want killer benefits and professional growth. They want to be surrounded by teammates who give a shiitake and are proud of their work. They want a voice and they run from red tape. Millennials hate the "corporatese" and will see right through you.

While craft beer is a nice-to-have, they would rather sip it with their spouse on their back porch instead of in your break room. Snacks and a chef on-site? Well, while those are delightful too, this generation wants freedom, flexibility and trust over your perks.

Better yet? It's contagious. Millennials are teaching the Gen X'ers that there is another way and to accept nothing less. Rightfully so. Which begs the question, what are you on the frontlines of human resources and recruiting going to do about it? Just wait until you meet someone who has already had a taste of great. Not good, I said great. It's an entirely different ball game. Get ready, be ready. The new era is here and our mission is to keep up.

CHAPTER TWO

WHAT IS CULTURE DRIVEN RECRUITING AND WHY SHOULD YOU CARE?

"If you hire people just because they can do a job, they'll work for your money." But if you hire people who believe what you believe, they'll work for you with blood, sweat and tears."- Simon Sinek

The American Psychological Association estimates that more than $500 million is siphoned off the profit margin from the U.S. economy because of workplace duress, and 550 million workdays are lost each year due to people crumbling under stress and pressure.

I don't know about you, but I could make some things happen with that kind of cash and a few extra days in the year...Starting with packing us all on a plane to Bora Bora for a stiff coconut cocktail or two.

Although more difficult to quantify, the cost of disengagement is just as if not more, disgusting.

In studies by the Queens School of Business and by the Gallup Organizations, disengaged workers had 37% higher absenteeism, 49% more workplace accidents, and 60% more errors and defects in their work product. In organizations with low employee engagement scores, they experienced 18% lower productivity, 16% lower profitability, 37% lower job growth, and 65% lower share price over time.

I can throw troubling stats at you all day, but the moral of this story is that stressed and checked-out employees are expensive in more ways than ten. I can guarantee you they won't be doing any recruiting for you. A disengaged employee is far more expensive than investing in professional development and talent cultivation, but we will dig into that in the pages ahead.

Good news, the solution is delightfully simple. Your teammates want to feel valued, supported, secure and respected. Make that happen and everyone in your professional squad will be happier, healthier, productive and, most likely, more profitable. Make that happen and the recruiting is no longer your biggest impediment. Your teammates who feel valued and excited are sending only the best of the best your way because they truly want to work next to them again. There is no talent war if you eliminate the competition.

Let me tell you about a client who has done it well and a client who experiences tons of turnover for all the right reasons.

Let's start with client X. Client X has tons of funding, an epic product and is in dire need of a software development team to help build out their life-changing product in the automotive industry. Building a stellar team is vital to their success. They can't move forward without the staff to pull into that parking lot every Monday. Their product now becomes their people.They can have all the money, all the ideas, competitive pay and great benefits but without the staff they have their hands tied. I worked with client X to fix their culture not build it from scratch. Their turnover was high and they hadn't the first clue why they couldn't keep talent. After the initial assessment of the organization, most of what I was seeing included a highly dysfunctional executive team and employees in roles that were way over their head. Your typical start-up, right?. Everything stems from the top so if your executive team is made of up of all the wrong talent then the rest of the organization is going to have a hard time thriving. Second, they had created an environment where new ideas were never heard and sometimes if delivered on the wrong day you could be fired. In an organization of less than one hundred people, everyone was afraid to speak about anything including really big decisions. The CEO had no experience in software and had a hard time letting his technical team run with the decision making. He reminded his top employees that they were replaceable weekly and constantly threatened their jobs. Talking about personal information or your family life at work was forbidden. The air was so thick it was polluting the employees. Working from home was frowned up because the leadership wasn't mature enough to trust their own employees.

Next, I interviewed the HR team. The Director of HR was inexperienced and overwhelmed... When I approached this director about the turnover that was happening she got extremely defensive and blamed everyone in the organization individually.. No one on the leadership team could take any blame. The maturity level was not where it needed to be.

I wasn't sure there was hope for this place if I'm being 100% honest. I continued to work with them for the next year. We brought on new hires and grew the team. I spent countless hours working with HR to revamp their entire recruiting process from the ground up. We worked on the onboarding experience for new hires as well and crafted a stunning in-boarding process hoping to regain some retention. I met with all the staff individually to get their take on the culture, and the executive team. Let's just say it wasn't pretty. They were on the verge of losing all of their staff. The common theme was that everyone was staying because the pay was so good, but as soon as something better comes along they were out of there, even if it meant lower pay.

Bringing my collective findings to the executive team was not a fun day.They rejected all the feedback and blamed every employee individually for different reasons. These engineers were stellar and had stunning resumes to back that up. I was so dissapointed knowing that I might not be able to help this organization at this crossroad. Company parties were not a thing, lunch breaks were monitored daily, freedom was out of the question, trust was a forgotten term, and they expected everyone to be glued to their cube. It was turning into the most toxic place I had ever stepped foot in. Being on-site more than once a week was killing me as an outsider so I can only imagine how the team members felt.

The end of the story for Client X is unfortunately, not a happy one. I ended up having to let them go as a client. They were making zero progress, continued on with crazy amounts of turnover and had no desire to fix the culture they had bred. They never understood that their people were in fact their product. Sometimes you cannot win them all. Today they are down to a highly disengaged skeletal crew.. They can't hire anyone because Glass Door, and Google reviews have tarnished their outside reputation. You cannot win them all. That's when you know it's just time to walk away and it's okay. Leave em high and take the high road.

So, let's find the positive here. Meet one of our client's here locally in Charleston, Client Y who is on the path to greatness. The CEO is a female and has built a software that is super cutting edge. She is a badass in every way. She built her culture from day one knowing that her product was never her software platform. Her product was her people. Again, if you have noone showing up on Monday than you have nothing. There is no talent war if you eliminate the competition.

The CEO at client Y has built a place where people want to show up. Their families are valued, their life outside of work matters, their professional growth is key and they are given trust and freedom to live their best work life. The CEO set up a platform for her team members to be successful. She knows if she pours into them they will work even harder for her. She pays competitively and offers awesome benefits. She is on top of her employee engagement. She does thirty day check-ins with her managers and team members and has a pulse on what is working and what is not. She created an on-boarding experience that people talk about over dinner with their peers and family members. She offers unique professional growth opportunities and is sure that her team members are happy and fulfilled. She plans family outings as a company and wants to see her team members succeed.

This CEO allows her team members to work from home when they need or want to, she pushes them to grow professionally. She has created a safe environment where white elephants don't exist. Her team does most of her recruiting for her because they love where they work. She has a waiting list of folks trying to get in at the ground level. Her recruiting model is working. The talent is coming to her. Her team members recruit people they want to work next to. It works. She is spending very little money, time or energy on recruiting. Her team is very protective of their amazing work space and so they don't just let anyone in. It's magical really.

As a leader, she loves feedback. She can handle it and embraces it whether it is good or bad. As a leader, she sees all feedback as a way to grow. She creates an environment that is judgement free and diverse. She promotes over-communication and sees the value in diversity. This CEO has loyal employees and it's because she understands that employee engagement cannot be bought; it must be earned.

This CEO will soar. Her turnover will continue to be low or non-existent and the way her customers are treated by her happy employees will be otherwise unheard of.

I can feel your eyebrow raising from here. "Cool story, LA, but how, do tell, do I turn this worm?"

First, you must shift your thought process. Do some research. Check out the NetFlix and Zappo's cultures and then find the small guys who are doing it too. Ask them to share their journey with you and why this kind of recruiting works for them. Everyone has a different journey and you will learn something new each time you hear another's highs and lows.

Hiring on culture first isn't hard. Hire for your culture. What is your culture? What do you want your culture to be? Write these down before we go any further. Don't stress they can be ever changing.

Mark my words, this equation will ultimately increase your retention rate and allow you to hire long-term team members that are not only invested but engaged. Invest in hiring the right talent the first time - pays off in spades.

Why do you care? I dare you not to care! You will be left behind, trust me my friend. You will suffer high turnover, disengaged employees, and the survivors left will only be there for a paycheck because they are C-players.

CHAPTER THREE

WHERE DO I START? BEGIN WITH WHAT MATTERS - YOUR VALUES!

"In matters of style, swim with the current; in matters of principle, stand like a rock."- Thomas Jefferson

Starting at the beginning is a perfect place to start! Breaking the seal is by far my favorite hurdle because if you do it, you are already leaps and bounds ahead of your colleagues and your competition.

Real talk, you are likely coming from one of two places: neck deep in a broken culture suffering from high turnover, losing people left and right, or you are brand new to this game and desperate for guidance in tackling your recruiting efforts head on the first go round. Take a deep breath. This is way easier than you might think.

Get a pen and paper ready for the next few chapters. You heard me, a pen and paper. Or colored pencils because why not?

Let's take a temperature check on your culture first. Maybe you don't know where your culture stands in comparison to other companies in your industry. Perhaps you feel something is off, but aren't sure how much it should worry you. Maybe you know your culture could be better but you are uninspired. Let's start with a quick exercise to get your grey matter firing!

Some of these might be hard to answer. That's the idea. Dig deep. Don't give up. Keep going, the best recruiting is right around the corner. However, first we tackle the groundwork.

If you were interviewing at your organization what would attract you to the company? Why would you be excited to work at your organization?
Why does your organization exist? What problem is your organization solving?
When you make a new hire, what soft skills are you looking for?

Describe your company in three words.

Describe your company culture in three words.

What does culture mean to you? Define it in your own words.

When you wake up in the morning, what excites you most about going to work?

What about your organization keeps you up at night?

What/who was your most successful hire and why?
Who are your biggest competitors and what sets you apart from them?
If you could change one thing about your organization today, what would it be?

Whew. Give yourself a high five or pour a glass of wine because finding words for those questions isn't much of a picnic.

Now, let's talk about the framework of your fortress. Core company values. Yup, sounds as cheesy as it is. Get over it. You will have core values as everyone does...or really should.

Core company values are just as essential as personal values. (If you don't have those either, get on that like white on rice)

You need core values to hire on culture first - just as much as you need a strong framework to support finishes. If I were you, I wouldn't hire a single soul until these values are written down - shall it be written, shall it be so. Once you have identified your core values as an organization it is your responsibility to post them everywhere. Everywhere! Shout them from the rooftops.

Although they may not be set in stone from now until the end of time, they should be your corporate guidance and have a presence in everything you do. You will use these core values as you hire new team members and develop existing ones.

An easy way to thin the applicant herd? Anyone that joins your organization must align with your core values - if they do not, this is not the role for them. Period. Why? Because if they don't align with your core values today, they will leave tomorrow. Trust me.

Do as I do, not just as I say, here are the core values for OIAM. You can find them front and center on our website. Why? To steer away people who don't align with us and to excite the ones that do!

1. **Fight mediocrity**
2. **Don't be an a**shole**
3. **Shared success**
4. **Do the right thing**
5. **Take ownership**

Bringing this full circle, here are my core values as a human:

1. **Honesty is the only way.**
2. **Be kind to everyone. Just be nice.**
3. **Forgive so quickly, the alternative is awkward.**
4. **Create an epic life for those around me.**
5. **Grow personally and professionally at least once a day.**
6. **Do what is right even when it is the harder more lonely path.**
7. **Lead by example, always.**

See how those two camps align? Again, we are human beings living and working beside other human beings. If your personal values do not align with company values that ship just won't sail. Life is short, you don't have time to be trapped in the wrong job surrounded by people you don't align with.

Your turn, get out that pen!

What are your organizations core values?

What are your own personal core values?

Pro tip, anything you list should be deal-breakers both personally and professionally. If they don't all pop in your head now, come back to it. Don't write any down that doesn't give you all the feels.

Okay, I'll get in the hot seat. Let's use OIAM's core values as an example. If I were bringing on another team member, whether it be a leadership partner or front desk receptionist, you bet your britches these values are in the back of my mind with each question asked ...and I am listening intently to the candidate's response.

Are they fighting mediocrity or are they just getting a paycheck in their current role? Is this person proud of their work? What examples have they given me to prove that they are proud of their work? Are they getting along well with their team or are they the cog in the wheel? Are they the one stating the obvious on conference calls (we all know that guy…) and eating up precious time, or are they asking meaningful questions and offering thoughtful insight? Are they focused on the success of others or just themselves? When challenged, are they doing the right thing over the easy thing?

There are an abundance of questions you can ask to cut right to the chase. As long as you listen, you'll hear it. The key to interviewing on culture first is listening and knowing what you are listening for.

Before you start running down the hall pinning people down for their personal core values, gear down big truck. You will not be able to boil an ocean. So, before we go any further let's remember to pace ourselves - this is a marathon not a sprint.

An old friend and mentor who made culture driven organizations his passion put it best when he said, "I have put in my 10,000 hours and being an expert on corporate culture and employee engagement tells me, one-third of the equation of building a great culture is in the work environment. If you don't create a place people enjoy being, they will find a way not to be there. However, environment alone won't do it. You also need the people around you, day-to-day to be the right fit. In this case, fit means people that are enjoyable, resourceful, reasonable communicators, but not distracting or draining on personal energy." - John E. Smith

CHAPTER FOUR:

BUILD AN EMPLOYER BRAND TO MAKE TALENT SWOON

"A word is a word, and a picture is worth a thousand, but a brand is worth a million."- Tony Hsieh, Zappos

Before you dive into this chapter, do me a favor. Call a colleague outside of your company right now. Not a friend - a colleague. Pick someone who you respect and trust to be transparent. Don't give this person a head's up. Start the conversation like this:

You: "Hi! It's <your name here>. Sorry to call you out of the blue. I have a question for you."

Admired Colleague: "Sure, what's up?"

You: "I need you to be completely honest with me here. Don't hold back. You ready?"

Admired Colleague: "Probably not. But shoot."

You: "You are at dinner with a friend and they mention an opportunity they are seriously considering with my company. They want your opinion on us - what would you tell them? Give it to me straight aaaaaand go!"

Do this exercise with at least 6 trusted colleagues and take stock. Surprised? Wounded? Elated?

This quick poll is an excellent way to gauge your employer brand and understand how others view your organization.

"But wait, LA, I thought this was a book about recruiting. Why are we talking about branding...isn't that something my marketing department should handle?"

Yes and no. Employer branding is not just for your marketing department, folks. How your organization presents itself as an employer is a whole new ball game than how your brand shows up to entice prospective clients or customers. Although the two should align, the motivations are different. Employer branding isn't about selling your product or services, it's about selling your organization as THE place to thrive - where innovative things are happening and dreams are coming true day in and day out.

Did your colleague's response give you the tingles? If not, how do you hope to make your industry's leading talent weak in the knees over working with you?

The stability of your house is only as good as it's foundation. Your mission, should you choose to accept it, is to cultivate a culture that not only inspires internally, but also shows up as the creme de la creme in a noisy job market. You accomplish this by becoming the employer of choice. If you have a stellar employer brand not only will it do the recruiting for you but it will also attract only the right culture fit. Think of this as an efficient out of the box new way of recruiting. Think about this too, imagine having a solid pipeline of ridiculous talent that your team referred just waiting to get in your door? Yes, calm down, this is doable.

What is an employer of choice you ask? Think Chik Fil A, Google, Starbucks, Apple, Disney, Amazon, or Zappos. Although you may not know the in's and outs of their products or services, you KNOW who they are, that they go their own way, and talent wants to sit at their coveted table. There is no talent war, if you eliminate the competition.

In addition to a baller brand identity to begin with, you also have insight into their company culture. Love it or hate it, they stand for something, they don't look like anyone else, and you have a strong sense of what it would look like to be on their team.

Back to you, building a strong employer brand starts with taking honest stock of how your company is perceived by prospective talent today. You've asked the hard questions and can also do some digital research into how you show up across platforms and social channels.

Here is the thing about social media. You can hide ..but not for long. If you are in the art of recruiting than you know that tons of our client leads, candidate leads and recruiting events come from social media. If you are a recruiter getting ready to retire than you can skip this chapter. If you do not find yourself in the retiree category than you better listen up. Social media can make or break you right now whether you want to accept that or not. You said you wanted to automate recruiting as much as you can without depleting the human aspect right? Well, then you better come damn near close with optimizing social media the best you can. Nobody buys a product anymore without reading the Google reviews. The same goes for job hunting, nobody with a brain applies for a job without stalking the Google Reviews and Glass Door reviews to be sure what is out there on the interwebs aligns with what they are looking for. Ask any of our recruiters and they will tell you that 95% of our talent comes from passive sourcing..mostly social.

To help, here's a quick punch list - put yourself in the shoes of talent-on-the-prowl and rank how your company shows up:

Platform/Channel	**Employer Brand Score 1-10 (1= they may egg our cars to 10= they love us, they really, really love us)**
Company Website	
Google Reviews	
Glassdoor	
Company Blog	
Yelp	
Facebook	
Instagram	
Twitter	
Corporate Responsibility	
GitHub	
YouTube	
Community Involvement	
LinkedIn	
Google Reviews	

Now switch gears, how do you WANT to show up? What do you want those purple squirrels to know about the organization you love so much? Why would people want to work at your organization? What are they wrong about or missing?

Here's where you call in the marketing gurus. Assuming a candidate worth their salt will want to do about 80% of their research on you independently before applying, here are five ways to step up your employer brand and marketing game from our friends at Front & Center:

8. **Craft your pitch -** similar to your company's elevator pitch, but targeting prospective candidates. Make sure that messaging is consistent across your materials and social channels.

9. **Give them something to talk about -** share employee features and spotlights across your social media platforms and blogs. Talk about rising stars, community activists and team wins. Not only will this peak a candidate's interest, but will work internal moral wonders too. Use humans! No stock photos!

10. **Add or revamp your careers page on the company website.** Make sure it's easy to find, navigate and gets people jazzed. No corporatese, outdated openings, or broken links here.

11. **Develop a posh employee benefits presentation and printed pitch package.** Think something slick and compelling designed to make prospective talent drop everything and sign your offer letter.

Remember, you want the best of the best so make sure they know it.

12. **Run campaigns for your open positions like you would a lead-generating marketing campaign.** Be smart, have a strategy and SELL that role.

Social Recruiting Is:	Social Recruiting Is Not:
Getting out and meeting humans. Socialize! #hashtagallthethings	Only hiding behind the screen. #dontgocrazyonthehashtags
Listening to what people crave. Contribute.	Mass emailing and spamming candidates.
Being pro-active all day everyday!	Guerilla marketing without any plan or objective.
Building out fabulously creative sourcing templates that are targeted.	Sending generic LinkedIn templates.
Keeping up with old candidates via all social media channels. Keep that pipeline strong!	Using "job portal language." Don't do it!
Maximizing the referral process by leveraging your network.	Relying on job ads and applicants. No, "posting and praying!"
Finding innovative topics to discuss with your audience. Engaging your audience.	Is not cutting and pasting the first Inc.com article you can find.
Creating a blog on your site for your followers to keep up on the latest industry trends.	Retweeting and reposting. Be original.

Selling your jobs through social media and using SEO and Google analytics to target your exact audience.	Cheap looking. Put some bucks behind it!
Setting realistic goals for your team to achieve.	Thinking you will have thousands of followers overnight.

I advise you to check out our social media! We pride ourselves in our social recruiting and we are super proud of our content. Feel free to steal anything you want! #opensource

There are so many benefits to social recruiting. Here are a few to get started with and jazz you up!

Increased Access to Talent – If you are not messaging your candidates on Facebook you are slowing your own process down. Maybe a few years ago that was not professional, now it is. There is nothing like hitting up a fresh candidate or good ole Peter from your pipeline while he or happens to be in the Starbucks drive thru trolling Facebook anyway. Be where your candidates are.

Ask your Fans to Give Back – If you have client's that are super happy or candidates that are super thrilled ask them to help you by leaving a Google review. Why not? We take ours very seriously, check them out (oneinamil.com). More often than not, we get new candidates and new clients because they saw our Google reviews and they can see that we stand out from the crowd. Make it happen and set goals. Each month set a number that you hope to hit for new Google reviews.

Low Cost – Social recruiting can be so effective and so cheap. All accounts are free to create and tapping into a targeted "boost" on Facebook can actually be fun. Save your dollars for posting your jobs on LinkedIn etc. Use your social dollars wisely because you don't need many. Each Monday create a strong social recruiting plan for the week. Set yourself up for success.

Referrals and Relationship Building – The nature of social media networks enables recruiters to make new connections daily. Those relationships can offer tremendous value in the form of referrals if they are properly sustained and nurtured. Long-lasting relationships lead to higher acceptance rates and more revenue for your firm. Make sure you spend time initiating conversations and getting involved in related communities in order to successfully build relationships and referrals on social media.

Passive Job Seekers – Passive candidates aren't necessarily looking for a new job, but they are highly qualified individuals in the workforce. Social media helps recruiters get in front of these types of candidates and convince them to make a move. By recruiting passive candidates on social networks, recruiters can tap into specialized skill sets and ultimately present better candidates to their clients.

Also, do your research, there is so much out there. Gary Vee puts it best in his latest $1.80 Instagram strategy. He says, "the truth is, the way to win on social media is to actually be social. The number of Instagram followers you have means nothing if you can't build a community of like-minded people who care and engage. The only real way to do this from scratch is to become part of the conversation."

You can find this gem here: https://www.garyvaynerchuk.com/1-80-instagram-strategy-grow-business-brand/. You're welcome.

Let's recap here, you've taken a look at your own social media and you have graded yourself accordingly. I hope you can stop and take the time here to compare yourself to others in your industry. Are you shining as a subject matter expert in your field of interest? Are you contributing? Are you creating a social community that people want to be a part of? Research your competitors. How are they doing things differently? Better or worse? Take notes and take control. There is so much opportunity here and it's up to you to make it happen.

CHAPTER FIVE

MAKING THE SALE...FOR YOUR OPEN POSITIONS

" Our job is to connect to people, to interact with them in a way that leaves them better than we found them, more able to get where they'd like to go. "- Seth Godin

Your mission, should you choose to accept it, is to find THE fit to fill an open role. At first blush, the position seems safe enough - staff accountant. Nothing too out of left field there, but you know better. You know it'll take the right type of person to gel with this special team and be successful in your phenomenal organization, so, already, the stakes are higher.

The prerequisite is to hire someone with the technical chops to get the job done, but it isn't just about getting the job done, it's, again, about finding THE fit, which will take the secret sauce of potential and personality to go with those hard skills.

Now, with all that in mind, I want you to go to your company's website, open up that careers page, and take a look at the "staff accountant" job you posted. Are you jazzed? Did it get you excited?

No? Then how the hot sauce is it going to get the attention of your cream of the crop talent?

Getting creative with your job descriptions is imperative. If you are looking for the one percenters then you have no choice but to cut through the noise and entice them. When a prospective new hire is reading your job description it should convey your culture 100%. A career move is a big deal for anyone. A career move for a candidate who is gainfully employed, driven, motivated and has plenty of adulting responsibility in tow is at a whole new level.

So how do you get those one percenters in the door? You sell. And you start with the job description itself. Take a look at the job description below.

Staff Accountant

Company Introduction

OneinaMil is a talent matchmaking firm, we specialize in culture driven recruiting. Our mission is to change the way traditional recruiting is done. We put human connection and culture back into the talent acquisition puzzle. If you are looking for "just another job," you've come to the wrong place. If you are looking for a new career, a job that doesn't feel like work, and you want to be surrounded by inspiring, forward thinking, high energy talent, apply today!

Who You Are

A Numbers Guru – you've got to love numbers. Our client is looking for that annoying person that pulls out his or her iPhone every 15 minutes to calculate the ROI on making your coffee at home vs. buying it at Starbucks, just because you are curious. They need you to do that pretty much all day, every day, but with way more important calculations that help move their business forward.

The "What If" Questioner – our client needs you to always be on the lookout for the next best thing or way of doing things – in every area! They are a company that's focused on moving forward, changing and growing, and they need you to be one step ahead of their ever-changing needs.

The Analyzer – a big part of your job will be analyzing numbers and translating them into English for those of us who are a bit lower on the IQ scale than you. They need help figuring out what those numbers mean to each of us and how our decisions and processes should evolve to meet our growth and operational goals.

A System Builder – as a growing company, our client needs new and improved systems. And by systems, they don't mean of the computer variety. They need processes that will scale and help them grow. Our client is looking to you to help build them.

The Penny Pincher – well, this might be a bit of an overstatement. What our client really needs is someone focusing on the dollars, and making sure they capture them, bill them, collect them, and spend them in the right way. Our client has tons of options and opportunities, and they need to dial in our decisions based on what makes the most dollars and sense.

An Excel Guru – do pivot tables and complex multi-sheet formulas make you salivate? If so, this is the job for you! Our client needs someone that can crunch the data and create the templates and figure out how to make us bigger and faster and better (yesterday if possible).

More Than a Little OCD – managing IT for small companies is like being the conductor of a symphony of details. Our client needs you to be on top of every little detail of their finances, making sure they're just exactly so.

What You'll Do

- **Accounts Receivable/Accounts Payable.** You'll be in charge of keeping track who needs to be paid and who needs to pay our client! You will be using our Service Management software to create client invoices, and QuickBooks to keep track of all vendor bills, payments, etc.
- **Client & Vendor Billing/Payments.** Easily the most exciting part of your job will be ensuring that billing is created, corrected/reviewed, and sent out in a timely fashion (okay, it won't be your favorite, but it's really important, and it needs to get done the right way). This includes responding to customer questions/concerns related to billing and the occasional billing disputes when applicable, and reviewing time entries for any bigger picture issues that may have arisen in order to head off any potential billing complaints.
- **Internal Reporting & Financial Analysis.** Our client is excited to have a number of reporting tools that you will be using to create any manner of reports and dashboards to assist the service team, solutions team, and management team keep track of their activities. You will also be creating and

using financial reporting tools and spreadsheets to keep them apprised of how they are doing.

- **Billing Administration.** You'll be in charge of agreements and invoicing in our client's billing system. This means truing up and truing down agreements monthly and annually.

What You Know

- 4 Year (Bachelor's) required. A degree in Business Administration with a focus on accounting/corporate finance would be strongly preferred.
- 4 Years' minimum experience in a Finance/Accounting/Operations role with significant growth/ownership over responsibilities required. Prior management experience is a plus.
- Experience with various reporting software packages is a plus. CPA is an even bigger plus.

If you're serious about this job, please tell us "why" you're the person we're looking for. We're looking forward to learning more about you! Thanks for taking the time to read our novel of a job posting. We hope you're as excited about this opportunity as we are.

What did you think? What I dig about this description is that it clearly conveys the technical skills required to do the job while also slapping you in the face with who our client is as a company. There is energy, there is sass, and you cannot get through it without a clear idea of what being part of our client's team would look like.

Moral of this story, stand out. Connect. Excite. And all of that needs to start with the job description itself as it will set the tone for the entire hiring process.

Once you've added the spice of life to your job description, where should it go? There are a plethora of options: LinkedIn, Dice, Ziprecruiter, Indeed, Monster, and more.

Shameless plug, add Workable to your shortlist. I am a serious proponent that every recruiter should have a tool like this at their disposal. We use this platform as our central applicant tracking tool in addition to leveraging it to manage our passive candidates and pipeline. How? The system blasts our open roles out to 50+ job boards helping us get our opportunities in front of, well, just about everyone. As a small army, not only does Workable keep us organized but it also helps us market and push our opportunities with a vengeance.

CHAPTER SIX
ASKING THE HARD QUESTIONS

"Skills are cheap, passion is priceless."- Gary Vaynerchuck

Now that we've kicked off your purple squirrel hunt, let's talk about what happens when those applicants start rolling in. This is the recruiter's time to shine: the interview process.

In my opinion, many entities go into an interview process with the flat-out wrong perspective. Their expectation is to be wowed. "Prove to me why you should be here." Which, quite frankly, is super arrogant. Times have changed, team. No longer is it acceptable to put a human in front of an interview panel to be intimated and demeaned. Down with the firing squad!

Interviews should be a two-way street. One that is paved with dignity and respect from both parties. Present your best and you will get the best from your candidate, which will help you both make the right decision about who is the best fit for the role. With that said, I challenge you to shift your perspective; instead of raking candidates over the coals, what would happen if you treated the interview process like opening your home to a guest?

This is your time to shine! Communicate clearly and consistently. Craft an interview experience to mirror the culture you have or want to have. Create a safe space to have a two-way conversation. Show your prospects their time and talent is already valued.

Often, my clients get hung up on questions. Any way you cut it, both parties need to learn a thing or two about each other, so below are some questions I like to use as early as the phone screening sessions to cull out the human behind the resume and, ultimately, sniff out culture-matches.

1. Name a book that has changed your life.
2. If you're life was a book what would the title be?
3. Tell me a time you had an awesome boss? What made he or she awesome?
4. What can your hobbies tell me that your resume can't?
5. How would you fly a helicopter full of peanuts?
    a. Make up your own insane question and ask it right in the middle of your list of normal interview questions. This will help assess the candidate's critical thinking and management skills. Do they ask too many qualifying questions or not enough? Is their solution in alignment with your core values? Crazy questions create a very real environment that the candidate can't prepare for.
6. How well do you adapt to change?
7. What are you passionate about?

8. What is one of your favorite memories. Give me the Cliff Notes.
    a. Get a feel for what someone values or what resonates most with them. Also listen to how they clearly communicate what is likely a long narrative.
9. If we asked your best friend to describe you in three words what would he or she tell us?
10. What are your 3 ideal job qualities?
11. If you won a million dollars in the lottery what would you do with it?
    a. It's not enough money to change the world or retire so see how their thought process works here.
12. What are your individual core values?

There are all kinds of cultural interview questions that can be asked. Our friends at Workable found this list to be super helpful:

- Do you prefer working alone or as part of a team? Why?
- Describe the type of work environment in which you are most productive.
- How do you prefer to get feedback from your manager: through formal performance reviews or daily/weekly meetings? Why?
- What do you hope to achieve during your first six months here? What would make you quit a job in the first month?
- What would you say or do to motivate your team during a challenging project?
- What's one thing you like about your current (or prior) job and you'd want here as well?

- Have you ever found a company policy unfair or inefficient? If so, what was the policy and why? What did you do or what would you do, in this case? Your manager assigns you a big task right before the end of the day. How would you reply?
- How would you change an institutional "this is how we always do it" attitude, if you felt there was a better approach?

Don't forget to tie body language into the soft skills arena as well. There are tons of ways to identify red flags or positive attributes all by observing one's behavior.

Once you've gone through initial screenings, let's fast forward to those in-person interviews. Let's assume you've narrowed it down to 3-5 top contenders who you invite to "your home" to meet "your family." Your work family anyway. Put yourself in the candidates shoes - what would make you feel welcome and confident going into this interview? I like prep-packets complete with a full itinerary, driving directions, LinkedIn profiles for ALL the people who will be interviewing them, attire recommendations, and anything else I think will help my candidate show up well. Set your candidate up for success!

On the day of, let's talk through arrival. Is your candidate greeted by a smiling face at the front desk? Bonus points if your receptionist knows the candidate's name. This may sound trivial, but the initial experience your candidate has walking through your doors is the first impression, so make it a good one.

What would happen if you treated an interview like an introduction? I will never forget going to a client-site a few years ago. The CEO called me pleading, "Please come in here and help coach my development team on interviewing." He went on to tell me this team rejected every potential hire, and, as a result, were falling behind on critical deliverables. I asked to sit in on a full day interview so I could better understand where things were falling apart..

The beginning of the day was great. The candidate was greeted with awesomeness. They even had breakfast for this candidate during his first morning interview. He was called by name at the front desk, offered something to drink, and given a tour. Money! We were on track.

Kind of. I then asked to see his itinerary for the day and he didn't have one. I followed up with whether he knew what his day entailed and he said, "No, I'm just going with the flow." Immediately, I knew this guy was so not ready for what was coming at him. Because I knew what the team had planned for him, I could already tell he was grossly underprepared.

After a morning full of bagels, coffee and kindness, he was put in a dark room with nothing but whiteboards. With no preparation, he was asked to code live in front of seven senior developers. He froze. He had made it this far without any warning that his introvert personality was about to be tried and tested. With every stroke of the marker he was challenged and questioned. After about 15 minutes of this blood bath, he got so intimidated that he walked out. Horrified, I took stock of the room only to see smug smirks across the developers' faces. I was not impressed to say the least.

Side note, this candidate was a rock star. He had proved his tech prowness with a six hour pre-interview test that he passed with flying colors. His problem-solving and critical thinking skills were off the charts. He went through numerous phone and on-site interviews leading up to this regrettable point and everyone loved him. He would have been an incredible asset to this organization, but instead went on to make magic elsewhere with a (well-earned) bad taste in his mouth.

A few weeks later, I was at a networking event trying to talk up an open role with this same company with a promising young developer. I barely got the organization's name out before he held up his hand to stop me. "No, I heard awful things from my buddy. Those guys get their rocks off putting people on display and tearing them down. Not interested" Circles are small, people. Whether you hire a candidate, your interview process is tied to your reputation and, trust me, you want that word on the street to be singing your praises.

This story has a happyish ending. I worked with the CEO to remove this part of the interview unless the candidate had plenty of warning. He obliged. Then we went on to tackle the next sticking point - that he was hiring pricks who were more interested in coming out on top than being part of a team.

But I digress. As an interviewer, you are doing a delicate dance. You are asking someone to consider making a significant life change to be a part of your squad, while simultaneously trying to evaluate whether they are the right fit for your role and your team. This is a tall order, but one I find you can best accomplish through common decency, transparency and personality.

Ask the hard questions. Welcome hard questions from your candidates. Give real answers. Be authentic.

Finally, when all is said and done, walk your candidate to his or her car. No, I'm not kidding. Leave everyone high! Take a look at your own internal interview experience. Where could you make small improvements starting today?

CHAPTER SEVEN

THE BIG KAHUNA - THE DECISION, THE OFFER

"You don't hire for skills, you hire for attitude. You can always teach skills." - *Simon Sinek*

It's game time. A hiring decision can cost you little or it can cost you a lot. No pressure here, champ. Making the wrong hire is bad for you budget, your morale and your energy. Let's try to do this right the first time, eh?

No stress. I've got you, boo. We start with the debrief. Following every interview, consider how you collect feedback from your team. Is it immediately following the interview itself why the information is fresh? Are you careful to make sure feedback from one person isn't influencing feedback from another? Tricky business that debrief, but put some standards and structure around it and you'll be right as rain. I recommend looking back on your candidate shortlist quickly following the interview and cracking the whip on getting independent feedback from your hiring stakeholders as soon as possible.

In my former start-up days, I used to go to my hiring managers' desk, pull up a chair and say, "I need feedback, start talking." I would type as they spoke to save them a step and speed up my process. Sometimes you have to do what you have to do.

Now you've gathered all that juicy feedback, collaborated with your hiring stakeholders and have found THE ONE. You are now ready to make an offer. Get excited! But make no mistake, this is not just about salary. Your top one percent will want more than salary - although money matters, it is not the only part of the equation. Your top one percent will want growth and opportunity. They want to be surrounded by people who invest in and challenge them. They will want to both learn and mentor. They will want an environment where they are trusted and their ideas are heard. They will want a work schedule that makes sense with their personal life, whether that means making time for travel abroad or a flex schedule to accommodate family time.

You have spent a great deal of time and energy getting to know this person. Consider what will matter most to them when putting together your offer. Make it count and shoot your shot!

When giving an offer, present the complete, polished package that outlines each and every benefit on the table. My two cents, make it a piece your marketing department will drool over.

To make sure you have all the bases covered, here's a quick and easy punch list for you:

- Send an email saying you have great news and set up the call
- Give the verbal offer by starting with "congratulations"
- NEVER give an offer via email
- Share the salary and full compensation/benefits
- Discuss start date and narrow it down
- Discuss a possible counteroffer and how to handle that challenge if it arises
- Have the hiring manager also call the candidate to welcome them to the team

CHAPTER EIGHT

BE THE RECRUITING MAGIC AND MAGICIAN

"A good recruiting process focuses and aligns recruiters to deliver the best to the organization. Ultimately, recruiting should really be viewed as a business partner, someone who is critical to the success of the business."- Matthew Caldwell, Head of Talent @ Instacart

Real talk. Greatness cannot happen without recruiting magic. Whether you are building a start-up or you have a 20,000 person organization, your recruiting has to be top notch. Repeat after me: Organizations that put recruiting first, come out on top. Organizations that invest money into their recruiting efforts, win. Recruiting, recruiting, recruiting.

Your people are your greatest asset - your greatest product. If you cannot get the winners in the door you ultimately have no product. Eye on the prize. Stay focused.

So what makes a good recruiter…nay, a magical recruiter? In my experience, I hire and train recruiters with three characteristics. First, is the ability to create and maintain meaningful, real relationships with candidates. This quality allows you to hire people that you have truly vetted and build a baller pipeline of solid candidates over the years. Often, I am hiring the same people twice in one decade. That is not from luck, people, it is from doing my part and keeping the relationships strong. Pulling this off takes keeping up with everyone's kids, new pets, new homes, the marathons they trained for and ran...and much, much more.

But you know what? It's all worth it. Stay connected to your candidates and the recruiting does itself.

The second quality I look for is confidence. In spades. As a recruiter you have to jump on the phone blindly and talk to just about everyone you can get to answer the phone. It's a slay all day or be slayed world, and if you are not bold you will not succeed. Recruiting is not for the weak. Getting on a call with a Sr. DevOps Engineer who is placating you because you don't know as much as she does will either break you or make you a better recruiter.

Finally. And this is the big one. The best recruiters do the right thing. Recruiting can be a shady industry. Am I right? More often than not, you will have the opportunity to take the easy way out. However, doing the right thing will get you places you will never go otherwise. Trust me. If you stay true to you, you will soar. If you give in, you will be a Shady McShadermiester with the horrible reputation in tow not just for you, but for your employer. Don't go to the dark side. Have faith. Look to the light!

Now that we've covered the characteristics you need to stay the course, let's talk about how you'll keep it all together with more than bubble gum and bobby pins.

Organization is key. Automation is key. Time is money, honey. If you are going to be cutting edge and hire only the best, you must be using cutting-edge technology. At OneinaMil, we use Slack, Workable, LinkedIn and every job site out there. We maximize our pipeline through our Workable applicant tracking system and we run our team similar to an agile software development team. Yup, you heard right. Listen up!

It looks something like this for us, but you do you, boo. By all means get creative and sassy:

Agile Recruiting Board

Requisition	Candidate	Testing
Sr. Dev Ops		
QA (Selenium)		
Sr. Accountant		Offers Pending
CTO		
Executive Admin		
Dental Hygeinist		
JAVA Engineer		Start Dates!
GoLang Engineer		
Director of Marketing		
Tech Writer		
Network Engineer		

Super simple, am I right? This model only works with clarity and transparency. Use the structure to hold your team accountable in a safe environment. Know where each candidate is in the process. Take time to celebrate those visual wins.

This model helps you see any gaps and where to redirect your internal resources. If you are not familiar with the agile software development process, just hit up Google and you will find plenty of inspiration and information! Running an agile software development team prevents technical debt and demands live feedback on a consistent basis in a daily stand-up.

Even as recruiters, we practice what is called a retrospective, an agile methodology practice. This is something you can do monthly, or quarterly to find out how you have done over the past time period and highlight what you have learned.

How might this look in practice?:

What did we do well as a team? Start with the positives. Here you can lead with wins - this quarter we saved X number of hours with Y new practice or go through some positive feedback you received from candidates successfully placed this quarter.

What could we have improved upon? In a smaller recruiting team, I love to have everyone come prepared with one thing they think they personally could improve upon and one thing they think the group could improve upon. For example, one might offer, "This month I personally dropped the ball on walking my candidate through the 'what if you get a counter offer' conversation and as a result lost a candidate very close to the finish line. As a group, I think we could do better about speaking up if we have extra bandwidth to take on additional requisitions." Everyone brings an opportunity for improvement to the table.

What impediments did we face? This is usually a time to share things that got in the way of you and your team achieving the ultimate success this quarter. For example, I might say this quarter one of my greatest impediments was not being able to get feedback fast enough from the hiring managers, which slows our progress down tremendously. As a team, I think the most crucial impediment we faced was the learning curve of the new requisitions that came through adding additional ramp up time.

What did we learn? Ending on an educational note. This is all about observations of the past that create opportunity for the future. For example, someone may share that not being proactive hurt productivity and ultimately slowed down the recruiting process. From there, we'd want to end with ideas and suggestions on how to be better tomorrow.

Make this work for you team - create whatever questions get you all to the same ending repeatedly and consistently. The goal of a retrospective is to learn from what you did in the past and either keep doing that or find better ways based on feedback given by team members.

So to recap here, I have put together a quick checklist for you to use in order to get started and maintain your agile recruiting team!

Agile Recruiting Checklist

- ☐ Figure out your automation tool. How will you keep your recruiting team on their feet when people are on the go and working remotely? We have found that Slack works well for collaboration and Workable is the key to an applicant tracking system.

- ☐ Create your "live whiteboard" so that whomever is in the office can run the daily stand-up using your whiteboard. Whomever is not in the office can dial in.

- [ ] Keep everyone posted! Sticky notes always work best for us due to the nature of how fast everything changes. It is easy to just move a candidate from one stage to the next. Be sure to put the candidates name and position on each sticky note as you move them around on the board.

- [ ] Replicate your whiteboard for those who are not in the office so they can follow along remotely via a simple Excel spreadsheet or their Workable Dashboard.

- [ ] Create your calendar invites for everyday at 9 AM and invite all members of your recruiting team. You must stay firm on whatever time you decide and stick with it. Therefore, there are no surprises and everyone knows what is expected of them at 9 AM.

- [ ] The goal of a stand-up is to define:
    1. What I am working on today
    2. What I worked on yesterday
    3. Any impediments I might have

- [ ] Put some light rules in place. For example, if someone is kvetching or rambling and goes over 3 minutes then they have to do a 2 minute plank. It keeps it fun and energized. Also, the point of a stand-up is to practice efficiency, transparency and accountability. So, think short and sweet!

- [ ] Lastly, pick your person who will be responsible for holding your recruitment retrospectives. Using just one person for this role works best. It helps if this person is super organized, high energy and engaging. If that doesn't exist on your team find the closest thing to it.

- [ ] Create calendar invites for you team and lock the date down. Decide if you want to do it once a month or once a quarter. Try to stick to the date picked if at all possible.

- [ ] You'll want your team to look forward to a retrospective so you will need to add some element of pizazz. You know your team best so figure out what the definition of un is to them. For our retrospectives, we switch it up with different kinds of food and a beer/wine selection. Sometimes it's Mexican, other times it's pizza. My team likes to sip and snack, so I know the way to their heart. What about kicking this party off with some recruiting trivia with Amazon gift cards for the winners? Or celebrating a killer time to fill month?

- [ ] Lastly, be sure to have someone taking notes. You'll want to send out a polished summary a few days after the retrospective so everything is documented and clear.

Also, remember if all these pieces don't work for you get creative and mix it up!

CHAPTER NINE

ONBOARDING - A FIRST DATE FOR THE BOOKS

"The first impression occurs at a subconscious level before your brain has time to evaluate the space at a cognitive level. It is felt, not thought."- Kristie Barnett

Put yourself in this position. Today, you start your new job - not just any job, but THE job. Even though you've set your alarm a solid three hours early (just to be safe...), your feet hit the floor before the second chime sounds. You laid out your outfit the night before - freshly steamed and ready to go, so you take a few extra minutes to cook yourself a healthy, hearty breakfast. All the brain food! You are ready. You have arrived. Look out world!

But then, something take a turn. You show up only to be ushered into an abandoned conference room where you sit alone under fluorescent lights with a stack of paperwork. Hours go by and no one has come in to meet you, let alone check on you. Nagging anxieties start seeping in forming a lead ball in the pit of your stomach. "Have I made a terrible mistake?"

Ever been here? We all have. Now that I made you relive that painful day, let's talk about how we do something completely different by creating a stellar on-boarding experience - the kind that keeps people talking and lines of prospective talent forming outside your door.

I want to start by disrupting your very semantics. Start referring to your onboarding process as an onboarding EXPERIENCE. Say that out loud. Doesn't it sound swell? Remember, there is no talent war if you eliminate the competition.

The goal here is to welcome your new hire with an experience that is on brand and on point with your company culture. It should be authentic. It should be personal. It should wow. It should have candidates sending you cake and champagne just to get a potential interview.

Yes, that last one has happened for me and my team. Multiple times. Live your best life, people!

More so, this is the only way to become better and faster at recruiting. Why? Because when you earn street cred for a stellar onboarding experience and talent retention, the recruiting starts to do itself. Say so long to those maddening nights of sourcing because you are getting back what you are investing in spades. Can you see it? It's going to be beautiful!

Ok, now that I've gotten you all hot and bothered, here is what you do. Start two weeks before your new hire's first day. Once you get a "yes" on that offer, pivot to going out of your way to make sure your candidate rests assured they made the best choice by far.

First, get the hiring manager to pick up that phone and personally congratulate your new hire. No emails and no texting - I said a phone call. I know, I know, everyone hates the phone nowadays but beas personable as you can be here and coach your hiring manager if need be. You are setting the tone for greatness and planting the seed for their future relationship. You want these two to start on a high note, so make sure this call counts.

Leading up to your hire's first day, I like to think of it as leading up to a first date. Both sides are going into this eager and excited, but also with eyes wide open. With that said, put your best foot forward. My signature move is sending a surprise package with company swag, a giftie and a handwritten thank you note for joining the team.

Crank up the hype! Dig a little deeper on their personal life (but don't be creepy...) and understand the key players in their world. If they have young kids, send a gift card to an arcade or children's museum and encourage them to have a family day on you before they start the next chapter of their life. For some of my executive hires who were a bit harder to close, I have even sent an Edible Arrangements or a set of golf balls to the spouse of the candidate. You need the entire support system on board with this significant life decision. Have dignity, but don't skimp.

No one likes to be under prepared. Next up, equip your new hire with a full itinerary for their first week. Give them a detailed calendar of where they will be when. This little bit of insight gives them time to mentally prepare and also come up with questions they want to ask specific individuals. Transparency is always appreciated. Over communication is the only communication. Be sure to add one-on-one meetings with leadership to the agenda as it is important for them to invest the initial time into the new hire.

Arm your team. Send out an email ahead of time to all of your staff breaking the exciting news about all the new hires. Include pictures and bio's of each person coming on board. Be sure to add the new hire's LinkedIn profile. Nothing is more welcoming than getting an overwhelming amount of LinkedIn requests from your new work family. It also allows your current team members to put a name to the face and be sure they know who to look for at the water cooler and welcome.

If you followed my lead, you've already nailed the first two weeks leading up to the big day, but you are not done yet, my friend. The team member's first day is oh-so important. First impressions will always be first impressions - do overs do not exist and there is no second chance. Now that you have this candidate completely twitterpated, it's time to take things up a notch for the first day!

Questions for your consideration:

1. **Is the front desk ready to rock and roll on the candidate's first day? Do the know who they are looking for by first name and do they represent sheer positivity and excitement?**
2. **Is there a swag mug, notepad and fun pen waiting at the new hire's desk? Their new desk should be showered with whatever greatness your budget allows.**
3. **Is there computer/equipment hooked up and ready to go at their desk?**
4. **Have you printed out their agenda for the week and put it on their desk?**
5. **Is the new hire paperwork pre-populated with whatever information you have on file? Although**

necessary, this process is painful, so do whatever you can to streamline and take the edge off.

6. **When they open up their new laptop there should be a note saying something similar to the following:**

Dear New Hire (Insert Name),

Close your eyes and take a few deep breaths. Take another breathe and clear those lungs! The best is yet to come. We are so thankful and grateful that you have chosen us. From this day forward your life will be changed forever. Get ready for the ride of your life!

Thanks for putting your trust in us!

Cheers!
Your Friends @ X Organization

7. **Is the new hire's team ready to take them to lunch on their first day?**
8. **Have you created an epic non-traditional new hire orientation? More subjective, but think about your culture here - what is it known for or what fun quirks can you play up?**

All of those little, itty-bitty details really add up and the level of expectation will become contagious throughout your organization.

When it comes to the actual new hire orientation, go big or go home. Don't even think for a second about throwing up a bunch of powerpoints up and serving cold coffee. Just no. A swank, hearty breakfast will set the right tone. Get everyone mingling and talking to take off some of the pressure. Most new hire orientations suck. Make yours suck less.

Tell the story. Get the founders in there if at all possible and have them share the why behind their work. Everyone loves a good story. Get your new folks to buy in to what you and your team believe early on. Your goal here is to create a long-lasting relationship with a foundation built off of trust.

Make the new hire orientation interactive. Let's leave the cheesy ice breaking games at the door, please. You can do better than that. Have everyone talk about why they chose your company and what they are most excited about. Allow people to open up about their families and outside interests.

You've got this! I believe in you. Here is a quick checklist to hold yourself accountable:

The Onboarding Experience Checklist

Once Offer Letter is Extended

- ❑ Hiring Manager calls to congratulate the new hire and communicate next steps.
- ❑ Send a package to the new hire after the offer is accepted. The package contains:
  - ❑ Some company swag
  - ❑ A handwritten card welcoming the new hire and their family.
- ❑ Send the new hire an email welcoming them, providing necessary info or paperwork and ask them to send you a bio and some pictures to send to the team.
- ❑ Select an internal "Ally" to guide the new hire through their first week.
- ❑ Create a comfortable work station for new hire.
- ❑ HR coordinates a first day lunch with the new hire and a few team members (including their Ally).
- ❑ An agenda is created for the new hires' first week and is sent to the new hire prior to their start date.
- ❑ A few days before they start send an email to the company about the new hire with a picture, a bio, and pictures of the new hire.
- ❑ HR should reach out the day before they start to make sure they have all the information they need.

Day of Orientation

- ❑ Always start new hires on Tuesdays.
- ❑ Provide a small breakfast and endless coffee!
- ❑ Print their welcome letter, agenda & checklist
- ❑ Put a sign up in the front lobby welcoming your new hire. Make sure your receptionist and Leadership team know their name and time of arrival.
- ❑ If you have more than one new hire, create a fun, interactive icebreaker to excite your crowd.
- ❑ Give your new hire a full tour of the building pointing out people they should know and where the bathroom , lounge, outdoor space etc. is.
- ❑ Have your leadership stop by orientation and introduce themselves.
- ❑ Have all new hire paperwork pre-populated for them to fill out/sign. Do as much of it ahead of time electronically as possible.
- ❑ Group lunch (paid for by the company) on or off site is fine.
- ❑ Make sure their work station is set up. Include a note, some more team swag as well a little gift like a branded gift card for coffee.
- ❑ Make sure they know work hours./lunch hour etc.

CHAPTER TEN

INBOARDING- KEEP CALM & KEEP THE TALENT HAPPY!

"It's amazing what you can accomplish when you do not care who gets the credit."- Harry S. Truman

Remember the first time you bought a new car? You just loved that car and you couldn't wait to share every mile with it. You may have even given her a name like good ole' Betty Blue. It was a match made in heaven and the world was your oyster.

So, what might happen if you didn't get your shiny new car regular oil changes? Or if you never waxed her? Said to hell with tune ups and tire rotations? Your shiny new car would die a quick death… and may even combust on the side of the road. Yes, okay maybe I have been here before. Oops.

Point being, like all good things, even new team member relationships require time and attention. The difference here is that instead of sputtering out on the side of the road, if you don't tend to your talent they will up and leave you. Or combust. Either way, it's not ideal.

The honeymoon experience you created must live on and, no, it's not the easiest of feats.

The good news? I have tons of ways that you can hold on to that loving feeling inside your organization - keep your current team starry-eyed while making sure prospective talent is still busting down the door.

Fine print, this delicate ecosystem can only exist when you have functional, forward-thinking leadership in place. Here are some ways to do a health-check when it comes to your leadership team:

- **They empower.** Empowering means giving each team member responsibilities and freedom that allows them to succeed and grow. It also means giving positive feedback and constructive critiquing when necessary.

- **They delegate.** Leaders should never do all the work. If they do, they aren't leading as much as micromanaging, which creates a stressful environment. Alternately, it stifles learning, innovation, and productivity.

- **They are open-minded.** A leader should be game for new opinions and ideas. While not all ideas are good ideas, strong leaders create the space for their team to question, explore and test.

- **They take risks.** A good leader will take a chance to move the organization forward. Keep in mind, too many failures will negatively impact the team and the company, so take calculated risks.

- **They are always learning.** A key leadership skill is first to allow mistakes to happen in your environment (again, safe space) and then learning from those mistakes. As risk is a significant part of leadership, they must take the lessons learned from the mistake to make a better future decision.

- **They are passionate.** A leader must love what he or she is doing day in and day out. This will spread to employees inspiring creativity and productivity.

- **They trust their team.** They view their people as the company's greatest assets and trust these people to get the job done. This quality is all about building relationships among the team.

How did your leadership score? Six out of seven? Four out of seven? If your score is low here, we need to chat because there is some legwork ahead of you.

What we are aiming for here is a stage five organization. According to Dave Logan, John King and Halee Fischer Wright, authors of *Tribal Leadership*, Stage 5 organizations make up less than 2% of workplace tribal culture; however, it is in this stage when members who have made substantial innovations seek to use their potential to make a global impact.

Powerful stuff, huh? That's the A-team bringing their best game to take on the world. That, my friends, is where we want to be.

Unfortunately, the crowd at Stage 5 is small. Many of us fall somewhere into Stages Four to One.

> **Stage Four:** The transition from "I'm great" to "we're great" comes in this stage where the tribe members are excited to work together for the benefit of the entire company
> **Stage Three:** Crippling majority, 49% of workplace tribes are in this stage marked by knowledge hoarders who want to outwork and outthink their competitors on an individual basis. They are lone warriors who not only want to win, but need to be the best and brightest.
> **Stage Two:** The dominant culture for 25% of workplace tribes, this stage includes members who are passively antagonistic, sarcastic, and resistant to new management initiatives.
> **Stage One:** We don't talk about these guys. These are tribes whose members are despairingly hostile—they may create scandals, steal from the company, or even threaten violence.

By the grace of God, I was blessed to have experienced a true Stage Five culture. To be honest, I never started OneinaMil to recruit - I started it to help organizations build these Stage Five cultures with the diamonds in the rough. Talent matchmaking comes with the territory and is the easy part. There is, however, a debilitating acceptance for mediocrity - a mind-numbing assumption that "okay" is the best it could be. I refuse to accept that. I wanted to go out and teach HR and recruiting professionals how to make these competitive, mouth-watering cultures happen.

Remember, there is no "talent war" if you eliminate your competition. Your best defense is tending to your current unicorns so they have less motivation to leave you.

One of the fail-proof ways to accomplish this level of loyalty is with a plan and a path - a plan for your talent's growth and a clear path to get there. If you are hiring those one percenters, they will need to see this, and believe this, to stay on board.

There are various ways someone should be able to grow and flourish in your organization. A few of those top contenders are listed below:

Position-based growth

Motivated people who work hard would typically expect to move upward in terms of their position. If they do not see any potential for position-based growth on the horizon, it may decrease their engagement, and, in some cases, may be the reason they leave. Position-based growth keeps your top talents eye on the prize and eager for the next challenge.

Professional & Personal growth

Engaged and motivated employees seek the opportunity to enhance their skills and improve their knowledge - ultimately, increase their value as a human. People want to feel that they are progressing as professionals, not just in title but also in their arsenal. Personal growth matters too, and, I find, isn't often mutually exclusive (more on this in a minute). Your employees will appreciate that you see them as individuals and are interested in their dynamic growth and evolution as people.

Financial growth

Money matters. Financial growth is important to employees, as it is an indicator of their value and worth to the company — of course, they hope to increase this over time. Lack of financial growth is perceived by employees as lack of growth in terms of their own value for the company, which may lead to disengagement and even increased staff turnover.

As a general rule, employees perform best when the environment is growth-oriented, which is an essential characteristic of successful company cultures.

One of qualities that makes a Stage Five culture amazing is the ability to meld personal and professional goals into one. You want to be able to provide a stable platform for self-awareness. You want to focus on the human element of your team member. Are they in the right role? Are they happy and engaged? Are they helping their team members grow?

These are heavy questions, but are well-worth asking. One of the tools my mentor taught me is a sweet, simple self-assessment. I use the model in both personal and professional contexts. I carry it with me always and am excited to share it with you.

Start by filling this out for yourself first. See what you find. This alignment exercise should be an ever changing document as you continue to learn more about yourself.

Once you understand the intention of the exercise, give it a shot at annual reviews. Every year you should sit down with your team to make sure they are "aligned" in their role. If not, then something needs to shift.

Fair warning, this exercise is a game-changer - don't let the simplicity fool you.

****Instructions:**

Start by writing down all the things you are passionate about. What would you do for free? For example, swimming, organizing, public speaking, fishing, yoga, ect.

In the next column, write down all the things you are good at doing. You do not have to like this skill but you are good at it. As in, people seek you out as a resource for or to help them understand <blank>. For example, delegating, painting, rubix cubes, math, writing, editing, skiing, or even cooking.

In the Superpowers box, write down what you know you are a savant at doing. It is the role that you were put on this earth to contribute. It's what you do better than most others. Having a hard time coming up with a list? Then write down all the things that people might think are negative about you. For example, some people have ADHD and it might seem like that is a bad thing. However, if you look at it as a superpower than you turn that negative right into a positive. People with ADHD are high energy and can multitask like crazy. Their brains are constantly moving and they can sometimes fit a 19 hour day into an 8 hour day if they know how to harness that energy. Take a negative and turn it into a positive.

On the flip side, write down all the things you simply suck at. No shame or judgment here. For example, math, english, public speaking, ice skating, teamwork, leadership, being in social settings, etc.
Next, write down all the things that essentially drain your energy as a human. Anything you would probably outsource even if it costs you money. These may even be things you are decent at, but make you want to stab yourself in the eyeball with a spoon. For example, cleaning, editing, taking photographs, accounting, researching, ect.

Be honest with yourself here. This list is not what you WANT to be or what you are WORKING to be, this list is who you are today. The point of this exercise is to help you and your team members understand each other - to identify strengths and make sure everyone's path is headed in the right direction.

Want to take this up a notch? Have your team members fill it out and then share with 3-5 people close to them for feedback. Ideally, this group should include both personal and professional connections. Is their perspective of their strengths the same as those around them? Are they ah-mazing at something they haven't yet seen within themselves? Intriguing stuff, I tell you!

Passion

What would you do for free? What, when you do it, makes time disappear?

Well!

What are the things you do naturally well? What are your talents? What could you do almost in your sleep?

SUPERPOWERS?

Alignment Exercise

Suck@

ONEINAMIL

What are the things that you are comfortable saying you are not good at? What are the things you are not good at and probably not going to improve on?

- ______
- ______
- ______
- ______
- ______
- ______
- ______
- ______
- ______
- ______
- ______
- ______
- ______
- ______

Hate

ONEINAMIL

What are the things that while you do them you lose energy (even if you can do them well)? What are the things that drain you?

- ______
- ______
- ______
- ______
- ______
- ______
- ______
- ______
- ______
- ______
- ______
- ______
- ______
- ______

Alignment Exercise

Although an insightful annual review is a strong move, you need to keep tabs throughout the year. I am a big fan of the 30-day check in with each and every team member. This will help you and your managers see flags before they become fires.

These questions are structured so that you are able to get exactly what you need. Being proactive in your team members happiness is imperative. With the 30-day check-in, you will always know if you are about to lose a key employee and, most likely, figure out a way to fix it before that happens. #lifehacks

Overarching Goals of a 30-Day Check-in:

1. To dive deep into the candidates happiness and be sure they are getting the support they need.
2. To create tangible metrics around whether your team member is engaged or disengaged.
3. To build trust and a long-term relationship with the team member.

Team Member Name:		**Manager**	
Position		**Today's Date:**	

Give a personal share (make this about the candidate and allow them to share something positive that is going on in their life).

How are things going for you in your new position?
Is your role still meeting your expectations?
Have your team members been helpful? Is there anything they could be doing that they are not?
How is your workload (balance, comfort level)?
Is there anything you need that you aren't getting?

How would you assess your progress so far?
How has your onboarding been so far?
On a scale of 1 to 10 what is your job satisfaction? If it's not at a 10, what would it take to get you to a 10? Is there anything I/we as an organization can do to help with this?
Share a personal vent. This doesn't have to be work related.
Are you attaining your professional and personal goals for this quarter?

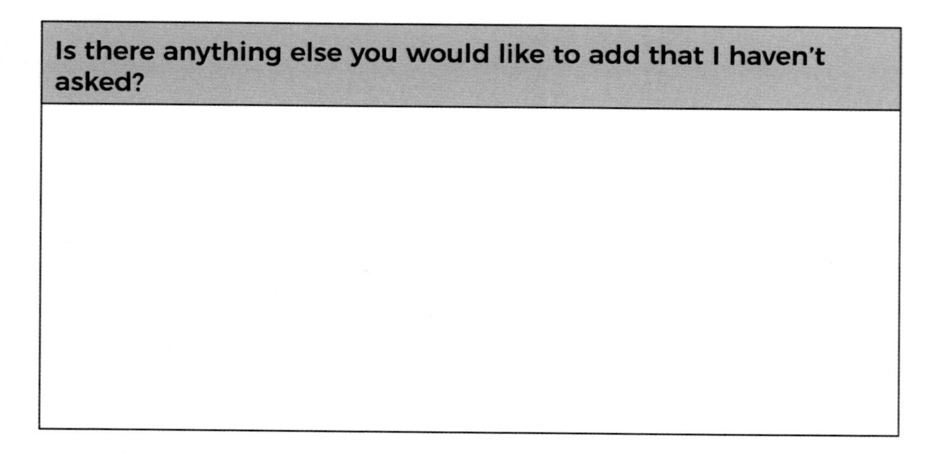

Is there anything else you would like to add that I haven't asked?

Now that you are armed with a regular check in and annual review tools, let's talk about what potential pitfalls you might be up against. One of the worst trends to plague talent retention, in the tech space especially, is leaning on perks to keep employees. Once the honeymoon is over, beer in the break room will not keep your star talent on your team. A candy wall or chrome panda may be cool, but what about competitive benefits?

Yes, perks are nice and do contribute to culture, but they are never going to be why people stay. With that said, ask yourself about the foundation and safety net you're providing for your most valued asset - your team. Remember top talent isn't only about that bottom line. They are looking for a full compensation package and often will take a lower salary for the right culture fit and stunning benefits.

Take a look at the environment. Keep in mind, you're asking people to spend the majority of daily lives with you in this space, so...what's that like? Is there quiet space for someone to step away and think? A nice outdoor patio for some Vitamin D over lunch? Looking outside the company walls, are you creating opportunities for your teams to chill

out and hang with each other? I like company-sponsored family events and "bring your kid to work days." I have also seen some organizations give a paid-day for their team to go out into the community and volunteer with their non-profit of choice. So inspiring!
Here is a big one - freedom, do your employees have it to work from home or on their travels? Is there support to take a mental health day or encouragement for self care after a stressful project? Opportunities for flexibility and freedom are probably one of the greatest selling points I have in my arsenal for top performers - they are the best of the best and will get the job done, so where they do it is trivial.

I'm throwing a lot at you, so, take a breath, and consider phoning a friend. A great way to keep everyone engaged is by creating a "Culture Team." Yes, this is actually a thing. You find the most engaged of your staff and put them all on one team. Give them a budget and ask them to meet weekly. The objective here is to spread positive vibes, get team members more involved and know that you have a crew on the ground looking for anyone who might be unhappy or disengaged. This group of folks will gladly volunteer their time because they love their company and they feel appreciated. I promise you, I have seen it action over a dozen times with clients from multiple industries across the nation. Start writing down a list of potential team members who would excel at this. They must be high energy, positive, mature, and ready to be the change they wish to see in this world. You know who they are, so go out and arm them!

Finally, consider HR Focus Groups. I can feel your eyes rolling from here... I know for most of us disruptors, rule-breaking, recruiting junkies this sort of jargon is the devil. I, too, felt that way until I spent the last five years on the road working with clients just like you and realizing that they do, in fact work, as long as they are done correctly.

Remember, there is no talent war if you eliminate your competition. That said, you must use your internal staff as your barometer.

Focus groups will help you gauge where along the recruiting process, from the initial phone conversation to the first day, there were hiccups or snags. Your recruiting or HR team should be running these meetings as often as possible and as close to 15 to 30 days out from your team members' start date. Ask questions to help improve your process and improve your employer branding. The opinions of those who have just gone through the process will be your best source of feedback. Remember to listen.

As you've noticed by now, I'm big on check lists, so here's another one for you. You're welcome.

The Onboarding Experience Checklist

Once Offer Letter is Extended

- ❑ Hiring Manager calls to congratulate the new hire and communicate next steps.
- ❑ Send a package to the new hire after the offer is accepted. The package contains:
  - ❑ Some company swag
  - ❑ A handwritten card welcoming the new hire and their family.
- ❑ Send the new hire an email welcoming them, providing necessary info or paperwork and ask them to send you a bio and some pictures to send to the team.
- ❑ Select an internal "Ally" to guide the new hire through their first week.
- ❑ Create a comfortable work station for new hire.
- ❑ HR coordinates a first day lunch with the new hire and a few team members (including their Ally).
- ❑ An agenda is created for the new hires' first week and is sent to the new hire prior to their start date.
- ❑ A few days before they start send an email to the company about the new hire with a picture, a bio, and pictures of the new hire.
- ❑ HR should reach out the day before they start to make sure they have all the information they need.

Day of Orientation

- ❑ Always start new hires on Tuesdays.
- ❑ Provide a small breakfast and endless coffee!
- ❑ Print their welcome letter, agenda & checklist
- ❑ Put a sign up in the front lobby welcoming your new hire. Make sure your receptionist and Leadership team know their name and time of arrival.
- ❑ If you have more than one new hire, create a fun, interactive icebreaker to excite your crowd.
- ❑ Give your new hire a full tour of the building pointing out people they should know and where the bathroom , lounge, outdoor space etc. is.
- ❑ Have your leadership stop by orientation and introduce themselves.
- ❑ Have all new hire paperwork pre-populated for them to fill out/sign. Do as much of it ahead of time electronically as possible.
- ❑ Group lunch (paid for by the company) on or off site is fine.
- ❑ Make sure their work station is set up. Include a note, some more team swag as well a little gift like a branded gift card for coffee.
- ❑ Make sure they know work hours./lunch hour etc.

CHAPTER ELEVEN

TERMINATION: SOMETIMES, IT JUST DOESN'T WORK OUT

"Don't be afraid to give up the good to go for the great." - John D. Rockefeller

It happens to the best of us. We go into a new relationship with rose-colored glasses only to have dreams dashed. The cost of doing business is occasionally making the wrong hire. We do our best to avoid this at all costs, but it will happen. And when it happens, the effort you put into how you terminate an employee is just as critical as the energy you put into bringing them on board.

This game is not for the faint of heart. From the HR side of our house, termination is in the air when a client calls with an "HR emergency." This is when I drop everything to help them come terminate said employee. This may surprise you, or sound cruel, but I love this part of my job.

I love it because the client thinks I'm coming in to help them get all their legal ducks in a row. Which I am and I will. However, the legalities I can do in my sleep. What I enjoy is transforming the traditional way of firing someone from that which so often ends in tears and nasty Glassdoor reviews to one that has the terminated individual sending you referrals down the road. Don't believe me? You will. Best part, It's actually quite simple.

Let's back up a bit. At this juncture, we have created a transparent environment from the get go right? Therefore, setting someone up with an ugly "out of the blue" termination makes no sense. If you are in the midst of a probationary period with a team member, be sure to document every meeting and every conversation. This meticulous approach keeps everyone on the same page at all times. Practice transparency. Embrace transparency. When expectations are set they become documented facts. You can't argue facts.

If you do this and it comes down to a necessary termination, honestly, everyone will be ready for it. I like to call this a "soft landing." Remember what your goals are here. You want to create a place where people want to show up. Why? Because there is no talent war if you eliminate your competition. Which does what? It helps you hire faster and more accurately. You want to treat people like humans. Even as they are on their way out the door.

Now, of course, there are exceptions to plans and transparency in this crazy ball we are on circling the sun. However, for posterity's sake, let's focus on the majority of terminations - those individuals who are failing to meet the essential performance requirements for their role over an reasonable period of time.

We will follow Jack. Jack is a software engineer who has not been producing. He has been on staff for a year and on probation for 90 days. Despite diligently showing up to every probationary meeting and trying to get his skills up to speed, he is underperforming and his underperformance is resulting in serious, expensive errors. From a business standpoint, you cannot handle the technical debt he is creating. He is costing your organization money. Sometimes, numbers are numbers at the end of the day.

Termination is inevitable, but now you have choices.

> Choice A) You could pack up his desk and meet him in the parking lot on Monday morning. Mondays are the worst anyway, right?
>
> Choice B) You could pack up his desk and meet him at his house leaving ample room for office gossip and speculation.
>
> Choice C) You could leave his desk, terminate him at the end of the day and offer to stay with him while he gathers his belongings and takes any personal files off his work laptop.

Which one feels kindest to you? Treating people human on the way out the door will allow that individual to self-reflect, own his or her circumstances, and leave saying, "You know what, they were great to me from day one. I would absolutely still tell my friends and colleagues to work for that organization. No hard feelings. They treated me with respect on the way out, they were grateful for my efforts, gave me a little severance to hold me over and even helped me with updating my resume." #leaveemhigh

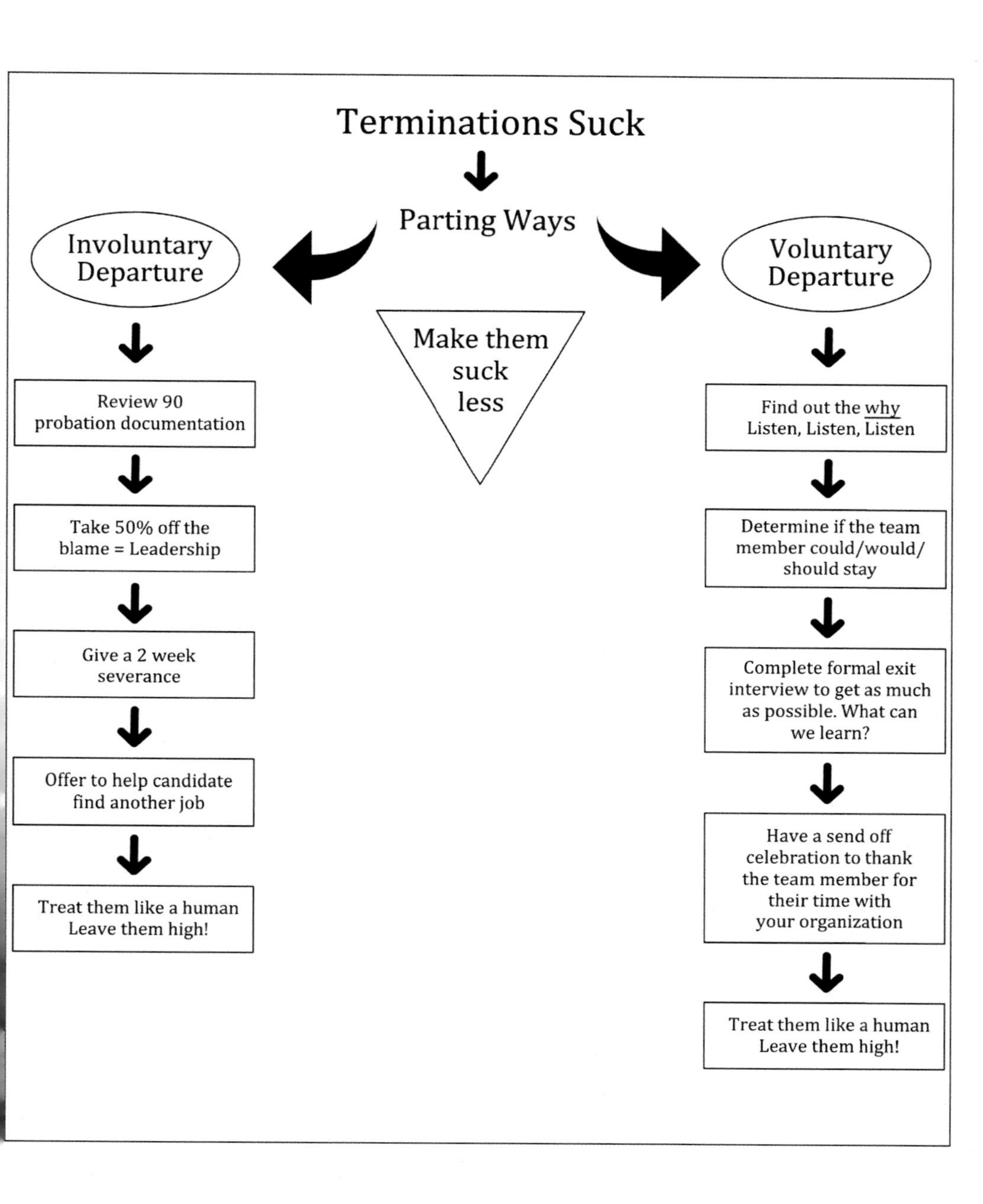
Terminations Suck
Parting Ways
Involuntary Departure
Voluntary Departure
Make them suck less
Review 90 probation documentation
Take 50% off the blame = Leadership
Give a 2 week severance
Offer to help candidate find another job
Treat them like a human Leave them high!
Find out the why Listen, Listen, Listen
Determine if the team member could/would/ should stay
Complete formal exit interview to get as much as possible. What can we learn?
Have a send off celebration to thank the team member for their time with your organization
Treat them like a human Leave them high!

CHAPTER 12

DEEP BREATHS: GOOD THINGS TAKE TIME...AND WINE

"You don't have to be great to start but you have to start to be great."- Zig Zigler

I have thrown plenty at you over these pages. Now that we've worked through the entire recruiting journey from soup to nuts, let's pump the breaks and talk about you. Wherever do you start?

This is a marathon, not a sprint,right?. All good things take time ...and wine. So pour yourself a big 'ole glass and work through this with me. We are about to break ground on a culture carefully crafted to bring the tier-one talent straight to you and make sure they stay there with gusto.

You ready? I know you are! Start by putting pen to paper on your first moves. Let's plan out your next 30, 60 and 90 day actions and goals to hold you accountable.

Thirty-Day Goal Setting

Sixty-Day Goal Setting

Ninety-Day Goal Setting

CHAPTER 13:
STAYING THE COURSE ON CULTURE

"It is the ultimate luxury to combine passion and contribution. It's also a very clear path to happiness."- Sheryl Sandberg

This is a long game it will require attention, upkeep, innovation and a pinch of creativity. I know where your head is - at this point, the questions are bubbling up in the back of your brain. What happens when I give my all to create the nirvana of culture only for these punks to get complacent and let it slide? What if we aren't actually that cool and never get to a culture worth writing home about? What if the air gets so thick in here people start choking?

Yes, these fears are real and understandable. I have been there, and have lived to tell the tale. You are peachy keen, jelly bean - just stay the course.

After the initial revamp, the shine will start to wear off your pretty penny. You may start noticing less teamwork, slipping initiative or zero stamina. People start going home early or stop bringing their kids by. You may even see an uptick in turnover and palatable shift in morale.

If you let things go on, soon you'll be getting the dreaded, "You keep losing the good ones." comment from an agitated customer. Now is an appropriate time to panic. But just for a second.

It will ultimately fall on your leadership team to pick up the pieces, but you will need to rely on your managers to be your eyes and ears in the field. This is especially critical for scaling companies - quickly scaling an organizationl is possibly the greatest challenge a company will face when moving from start-up to emerging. You will need all hands at attention among your leadership team as the faster you grow, the harder it will be to keep your culture in tact.

Working on your culture is a day in and day out operation. Staying ahead of the exodus starts with knowing where you stand. Take a second to jot down any HR-related changes that have come down the pipeline in the last 3-6 months along with a temperature check on how your employees reacted.

> Did you cut back on free snacks and sodas that caused ripples of concern over the company's financial health?
>
> Did you put a strict percentage raise model in place instead of celebrating individual contribution only to see a few top players slow their pace?
>
> Did you let go of someone who was well-liked but underperforming only to hear whispers about job security?

Have you lost sight of any of the following?

1. Freedom
2. Respect
3. Acknowledgement
4. Reward

You cannot hope to address culture without coming by the sticking points, and the reactions to those sticking points, honestly. Again, change and growth are hard, so no beating yourself up here.

Be sure to note what you think is going right too. Even if you feel it is a small piece, it is part of a large puzzle.

> Were you cc'd on an email floating around celebrating a team win - better yet, did the CEO chime in with praise and gratitude?
>
> Have three or four employees started training for a marathon together? Awesome! What can the company do to support and encourage them?
>
> Did a team member ask for continued education support and get it. Stellar! What can you do to help others make smart asks and follow suit?

Once you make your short list, choose two areas of focus: one sticking point that needs to be de-gooped and one warm-fuzzy that could use some extra nurturing. You won't fix this all in one day, so pace yourself, speed racer.

If you need a little inspiration, I have a gem for you to keep in your back pocket. This is an oldie but I goodie I use it all the time. Some of my clients do this every 30 days, some do this every 60 days, and others do it each quarter. Make it work for you, but stay committed.

Employee Engagement Survey - NES

10 Standard Points

Q#	Description	Category	1	2	3	4	5
1	Do you and your immediate manager have scheduled one-on-one conversations, which are focused on you?	Relationship	10	2	11	14	8
2	Are you recognized for your efforts (small and large)?	Recognized	2	16	7	9	11
3	How aligned is your passion and what you naturally do well with your day-to-day work?	Alignment	0	6	9	19	11
4	Do you feel like you are growing towards your personal and professionally desired career path and goals?	Growth	4	13	2	19	7
5	Do you feel like your opinion is encouraged, listened to, and valued within your organization?	Value	2	5	11	14	13
6	Do you feel like there is a sense of team, group or community in your organization?	Camaraderie	1	7	10	13	14
7	How well do you feel your organization communicates its values, current goals, and overall strategy?	Communication	4	1	5	15	20
8	Rate your overall average trust within your organization and the people you work with on a scale from 1-10.	Trust	4	2	15	9	15
9	How proud are you to work for your organization?	Pride	0	0	4	26	15
10	Rate your overall happiness, in both work and personal life on a scale from 1-10 (1= "Miserable, 10= "Happy")	Happiness	2	3	8	16	16
11	What would you change at Example Co?	Custom					
12	What is the most important thing we should be doing as an organization?	Custom					

Analytical Results

Answered	Wt. Score	Ne & Above	NES Score	Sum Low	Sum High	Average	Wt Score %	Ne & Above %	NES Score %
45	143	33	-14.0	-14.0	22	3.2	64	73	-48.9
45	146	27	-9.0	-9.0	20	3.2	65	60	-44.4
45	170	39	29.0	29.0	30	3.8	76	87	40
45	147	28	-9.0	-9.0	26	3.3	65	62	-35.6
45	166	38	22.0	22.0	27	3.7	74	84	20
45	167	37	23.0	23.0	27	3.7	74	82	20
45	181	40	37.0	37.0	35	4.0	80	89	37.8
45	149.5	39	19.0	19.0	24	3.3	66	87	8.9
45	191	45	56.0	56.0	41	4.2	85	100	91.1
45	172.5	40	34.0	34.0	32	3.2	77	89	40
							72.6	**81.3**	**12.9**

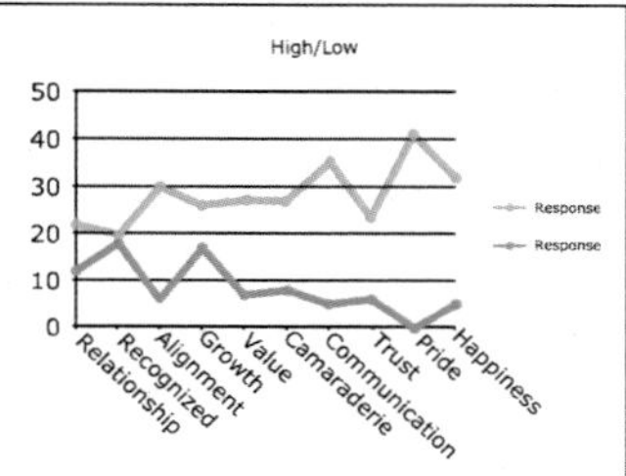

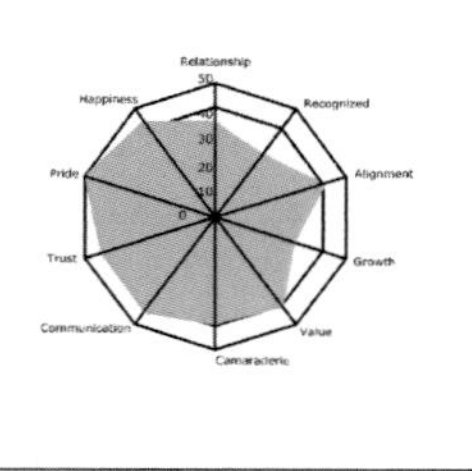

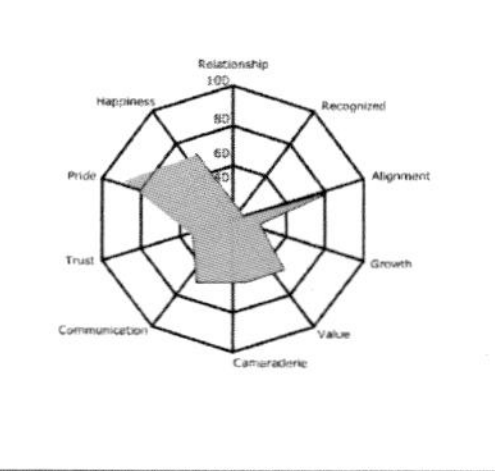

Info		
Total Sent:	47	
Received:	45	
Incomplete:	2	
Dates:	1/13 - 1/22	
Total Score:	12.9	<< NES Score

Human Context and an Overall Score weighted to True Results

NES 12.9

CHAPTER 14

LEAVE 'EM HIGH - YOU GOT THIS!

"A ship is always safe at shore but that's not what it's built for." - *Albert Einstein*

Page by page, you've stuck with me to the end, my friend. So I will leave you with one final nugget on your rise to culture driven recruiting glory - a pep talk. This journey of yours will have its ups and it's downs. Stay focused and believe in the process. Better yet, just start by believing in better, period.

Everything you've read is a result of years of trial and error that lead to both face-plants and wins. You'll probably experience your fair share of both and learn plenty of your own tricks along the way. This is all part of your journey. You have something incredible to contribute and I cannot wait to see you do it!

I promise you, what is outlined in these chapters has worked for me multiple times over, and I continue to topple and evolve organizations. There is a better way for us to work and you drive this change. If not for you (or me), we owe this to the next generation maybe made up of your own children or grandchildren. We all need to be living our best life both in and out of work. Evangelize my friend, it's importance is priceless.

Recruiting is an art. It can be done with such intention and impact. Let's commit to building those Stage Five organizations, the corporate culture nirvana, starting today. Let's continue to find outstanding talent and fight like hell to keep them. (My editor let me keep that one...)

I hope in some small way I left you better than I found you. Let's continue to strengthen our family of recruiters and usher a new-found respect for our craft. You've got this! You are in it to win it! And I am cheering you on from the sidelines.

Kick Ass & Take Names,
LA

Made in the USA
Las Vegas, NV
01 September 2023